Carbon

by

Elisabeth Kelly

First published 2022 by The Hedgehog Poetry Press

Published in the UK by
The Hedgehog Poetry Press
5, Coppack House
Churchill Avenue
Clevedon
BS21 6QW

www.hedgehogpress.co.uk

ISBN: 978-1-913499-65-5

A CIP Catalogue record for this book is available from the
British Library.

Front cover image © Frank Cone

We huddle together
held by such a
force
in this small
nucleus

Negativity
orbits
by

Contents

The atomic make up of Carbon

The Nucleus

6 Protons

1.   Your Laughter, 9
2.   Iron Lung, 10
3.   The Wood Worker, 11
4.   Haytime Picnics, 12
5.   The Common Periwinkle, 13
6.   Optimism in Winter, 14

6 Neutrons

1.   Collecting, 15
2.   The Fairy Circle, 16
3.   The Earth has Turned, 17
4.   Waiting for the Rain, 18
5.   Sewing with Mum, 19
6.   Sister, 20

The Orbitals

6 Electrons

1.   Memory, 23
2.   Night Owl, 24
3.   Little White Boats, 25
4.   She Just Nodded, 26
5.   The Brass Table, 27
6.   The Old Barn, 28

THE NUCLEUS

The centre of an atom, protons positively charged and neutrons with no
charge are densely clustered together.

YOUR LAUGHTER

There is a lightness,
an expansion.

Gladness settles around us,
like summer mist.

Encompassing, enveloping.
Still there later that day
when we touch the grass,
dampness on our toes.

THE IRON LUNG

Now as I hold you to me,
this first night when the world is
swirling past in echoing brutality,
the pressure in my chest increases
until alarms begin to ring,
red hands on gauges jitter alarming high.

It reminds me of a picture of a man,
in an iron lung I once saw in a childhood book,
fascinating the horror, of what seemed like confusion,
of chest crushing weight and an unbearable pressure to be alive.

They come to take you away so I *can get some peace,*
air compresses harder as breath falters in me,
the iron casing begins to vibrate with an atom splitting
power as I wrench myself from wire,
stumble down the laminated tunnel of cries.

Only when I have you back safe,
encased in my arms does the
tightness slacken to a dull weight.
A weight of love I carry always.

THE WOOD WORKER

The northern summer shines
its night light and I watch you.

Lean across feel your way,
assessing shape and warmth.

I see the future start to
flicker in your face.

Your inspection complete,
you draw the curved knife.

The newborn flesh gleams.
as the bark begins to curl.

The rhythm slowly settles,
over your whole being.

I am in the bedroom,
watching through the open window.
The sky is tucked in,
around the hills.

Your soft beat crosses the grass,
 and finds it way upstairs.

Unskinning, unfolding,
 enveloping us both.

HAYTIME PICNICS

Sweat blankets the ground as skin and grass start to crisp,
heavy cut seed dust settles over eyelids and behind knees.

We peel boiled eggs carefully untwist salt
coiled in tin foil, as splashes of Lilt sticks to stubble.

Together we jostle uncomfortably over the
Mr Kipling's Apple Pies exotic in their silver cases.

To soon the men unwrap their limbs from the ground,
head off back to the hay as we scatter crumbs like meadow grass.

I collect the foil packets flatten them out carefully
into shinny discs that catch the sun.

Place them later on the table by my bed so when
bruised clouds come I can see the sun.

THE COMMON PERIWINKLE

A treasure found, nestled in sugar kelp,
winking at you in the ageing sun.

You scoop it up, this empty home,
soothed by waves in its lonely sorrow.

What is it? your sea whisper caresses
the delicate twists, warms the burnished edges.

I see the shell has left, a brand on your
palm a stamp of our bright day.

A Periwinkle I answer,
nothing common about this one,
not today.

OPTIMISIM IN WINTER

In this cathedral of a city,
where the ceiling is made of
vaulted tenements the
roof opens to a sky of
ever changing density.

I clutch at my paper cup,
fingers blistering from the
heat battling the chill in the
Edinburgh air.

Like prayer cushions intricately
woven with patterns of
the past, the worn steps
tell me stories as I climb
through this place.

My heart lifts in exultation,
as I tunnel through the town.
I could raise my voice like
a chancel choir staring at
the stained glass of
the northern winter sky.

Like the angel sculpted in
the nave I want to lift up
my feet and rise,
face to the heavens,
arms free, stone lit
by the sun through
fractured clouds.

COLLECTING

The stillness of perfection,
a single moment when,
the circle completes.
For a second air seems
to shine like sun reflecting,
off cut glass.

It makes droplets like
autumn dew on webs,
that hang suspended in
softness and silence.

I pick them quickly,
one by one before
they fall, greedily
store what I can,
into our favourite jar.

Jumbled on top of
each other, a mosaic
of our moments that
builds day by day.

THE FAIRY CIRCLE

There is a place where the ferns do not grow,
the wood sorrel stops just shy,
the trees stretch out
roots dominate the ground.

It is here we see it pushing up through the moss,
edges frilled with neon the
colour of inside the sun,
petticoats of soft silk.

The smoothed domed heads invite me to
touch each one in the circle,
like a child counting stones.

You stop unsure,
You don't know the power it may have,
your voice like moths as dusk,
It might not let us out.

I look at the darkening moss,
the hawthorn trees reaching to each other,
Why would we ever want to leave?

I take your hand and together
we step inside the circle.

THE EARTH HAS TURNED

My eyes stride
across the open
hills searching.

Swirls of thistle-down,
like inverse snow falls
lift off over
the dying fields.

Wagtails stammer
from dried out
docks to seed heads
still in the
breeze free sky.

Weak clouds hang
over the farthest
moors blanketing
heather with fragile
droplets of chill.

A promise of
things to come.

WAITING FOR THE RAIN

The sky is bruised,
from jostling with the hills
all day.

The air has turned raw,
skin hums upwards searching,
animals stiffen as
silence shutters down.

Lane dust reaches a
swirling fist to
dense clouds,
falls back unchanged,
covering the gates with promises.

Alert,
confined,
we wait ,
still the rain doesn't come.

SEWING WITH MUM

We pin out paper like moth wings,
tack it safely to the fabric.
Ease out creases with quiet fingers,
the tissue so full of promise.

You work skilfully with practiced speed,
a Hawk-Moth gliding at dusk,
I flap against the cotton seeking reassurance,
my edges pricked with blood.

The pattern unfurls across the cutting table,
floating outward.
Your machine surges into life with
silver spools full of the future.

The rhythm of the peddle reverberates,
like the beat of a lullaby.
The form takes shape under your hands,
seeps across the wood.

A half-formed body is tucked around me,
final adjustments made,
edges smoothed I unfold,
emerge different
then expected.

SISTER

We used to picnic in the rain.
Do you remember?
Up by the old tarn, hidden behind
boulders on the spongey moor.

Even then we liked the drama:
the loneliness, the dreich, the softness.

I can remember the smell. Wet
summer moss, dug under our nails.
There even after our bath.

I could hide under my covers
later
and smell our day.

THE ORBITALS

A space where electrons, negatively charged particles, dwell.

MEMORY

My memories are like fish,
large glinting salmon casting
beautiful shimmers of
excitement through water.

Only ever glimpsed,
in quietening rivers,
where they flit and slip
from my inexpert hands.

But I was told once,
that salmon return,
years later to their birth river,
break the surface entirely
glimmering with hope,
as they leap home.

THE NIGHT OWL

The screeching night
flies past
my open window.

Seeking out the
hidden,
in furled grasses
with
nocturnal eyes.

It circles past on
silent wings,
my thoughts
gripped
by its talons.

The night becomes
shrill as
it picks over
my worries
bit by bit.

Then days later
they are reconstituted,
found in fur covered pellets,
in the soft woodland floor,
diminished by the day light

LITTLE WHITE BOATS

Rain that tastes of grass is falling,
fading away a ticket lost in the
mud outside my door.

Murky streams tug at frayed edges,
sailing away pieces like tiny
child-made boats down the garden.

I remember you in this flavoured rain,
a giant in this meandering world of tiny becks,
your dinosaur clad feet creating ravines,
as oxbow lakes form around you,
your laugh vibrating across the hills.

My memories flow with the little white boats,
floating away down the garden
washed by the summer rain.

SHE JUST NODDED

She just nodded,
as they came to her house,
cooked a meal in her kitchen ,
as if she hadn't held fancy parties,
huge rambling Christmas dinners.
Then they moved the table that,
had always been by the stove,
Fire hazard they said.

She just nodded,
as they moved her from bed to chair,
as if she hadn't once danced all night,
in skirts that swished like meadow grasses,
with clipped accented officers, whose
moustaches tickled in dark corners.

She just nodded,
as they packed her things, leaving
her son's old football,
the bound leather books with
her name along the spine.
The postcards from India,
that spoke of love between the lines.
Essentials only they said.

She just nodded,
as they moved her into a room
no dust and no memories.
Yet she sat and remembered dancing, making love,
knitting, cooking, holding, mending, soothing,
dreaming, arguing, debating, learning, creating.

And then
she just nodded.

THE BRASS TABLE

It stands in the corners like an unsure
guest at a too loud party wishing it could join
in with the coffee table in the centre of the
room or take refugee with the china figurines
on the hearth playing out scenes of rustic life.

The table glints in the sunshine as we play
Pelmanism with grown up playing cards,
the brass top polished with a cloth then with
Mr Sheen for a superior shine.

On it you place Mars Bars cut into squares
on paper doilies, leave reading glasses perched
near the edge as you rub your eyes,
reminding me of Mole from *Wind in the Willows.*

Now it is settled in the bay window of my flat,
half hidden by a cheese plant, I learn about
the cold sweep of Russian revolutions, how to
untangle the past.

There is a rumour the table came from India,
I stare at the dulled brass think of the velvet
lined box we found after your death that
snapped accusingly at my fingers,
of all the questions never asked.

THE OLD BARN

It is difficult now,
to remember the dark days,
stood here in the light of vaulted
ceaseless skies.

Walls of freshly painted trees,
show off their swatch card greens,
dusts laden seeds create a carpet
under our feet.

Strange to think of times,
when the slate roofed heavens
drips endless dampness onto a
cold stone floor.

When wind grinds like stones,
causes pointing to crack and fall,
drives rain like shards of ancient
window glass.

Now the sun warms the
emerald moss that decorates the mortar,
optimistic stems wave at the brightness,
no thought given to the coming night.

Atoms, you tell me
are 99% nothing. So,

we are all 99%
nothing. Yet,

you are my
everything.

ACKNOWLEDGEMENTS

Thank you to:

My wonderful family, Damian, Leo and Heather.

My parents, especially my Mum for all the Edward Lear and Robert Louis Stevenson that started my love of poems and stories.

The wonderful, encouraging community of poets and writers I have met in 2020-2021 who made me believe it was possible.

And to Mark at Hedgehog Poetry for helping me get these poems into the world.